The Bean Story

By Darlene Wierski-Devoe

Illustrated by Sydney Devoe

FriesenPress

One Printers Way
Altona, MB R0G 0B0
Canada

www.friesenpress.com

ISBN
978-1-03-830065-2 (Hardcover)
978-1-03-830064-5 (Paperback)
978-1-03-830066-9 (eBook)

1. JUVENILE NONFICTION, GARDENING

Distributed to the trade by The Ingram Book Company

Dedicated to my family.
Every day, you teach me how
to be a better human bean.

"Can I ask you a question,
my dear?"

"Do you remember the day we had all the little veggie seeds lined up, ready to be planted in our old garden boxes?"

"I was so worried that nothing would grow.
The soil just didn't look right."

"It had too many rocks and weeds and wood chips in it."

"There were **too many** things these little seeds would have to overcome to grow healthy roots."

"I even said out loud,
'This isn't going to work.'"

"I was so sure it wasn't going to work."

"You looked at
me with such
determination
and said,

'Well, we can always try, can't we?'"

"You said,
'Don't worry, I think it will be fine.
I know it will grow.'"

"So, we got down on our knees and, one by one, planted beans, tomatoes, carrots, cucumbers, lettuce, and even squash."

"When we finished planting all the seeds,
you looked at me and said with a giggle,

'It never hurts to try . . . right?'"

Hmm. "'It never hurts to try.'
Those words stuck in my mind.

It never hurts to try."

"After a few weeks of giving the little seeds plenty of water and saying kind words to them, they began to sprout and grow. The beans grew so fast. It's like they could hear us cheering for them!"

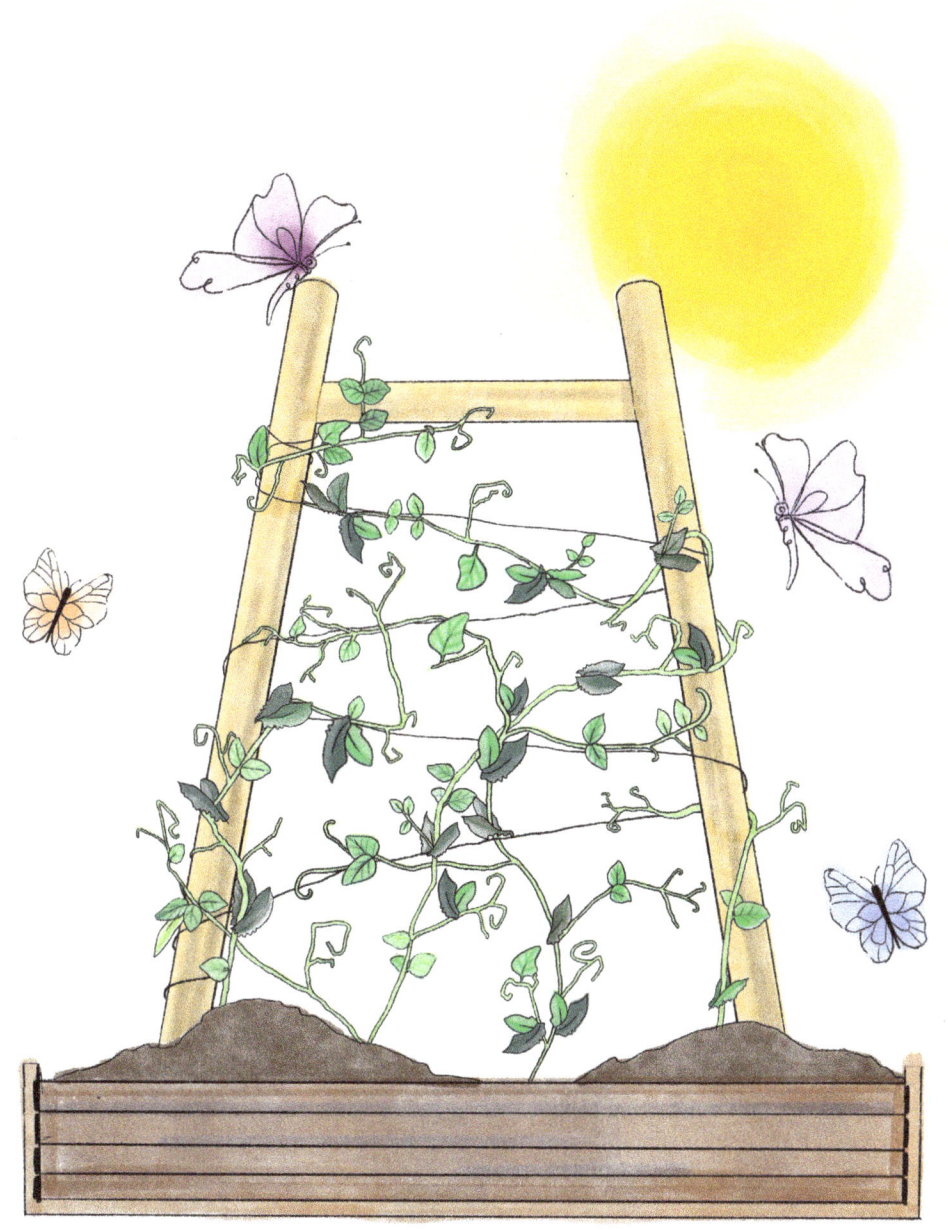

"The vines decided it was time to climb, reaching up the wooden stakes and strings. They grew bigger, greener, and taller."

"It wasn't long before

we started to see

flowers and buds."

"Do you remember what you told me? You said,

'I knew the beans would grow!

I just knew it! See, I told ya, I told ya! We just had to give it a try!'"

"I looked at you and saw wonder, success, hope, and pride in your eyes.

You were shining as bright as a star."

"I smiled. You were right. At that moment,
I realized we were both taught a very valuable
lesson by planting our garden."

"You know the feeling you
had when you knew the
beans would grow?"

"It didn't matter what I said or how much
I complained about the rocks, weeds,
and wood."

"You believed with all your heart that those veggies would grow.

Do you remember that feeling?"

"In a soft, unsure voice, you said,

'Yes.'"

"That faith—that knowing—that super-strong feeling in your stomach that made you believe with all your heart we'd succeed . . . that's how I feel about you every single day."

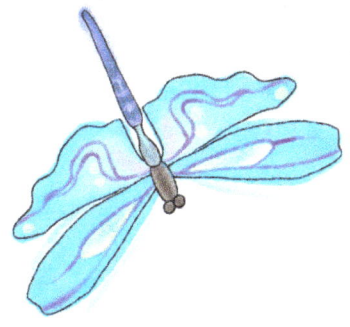

"I was filled with pride. I said, 'Even when things are tough, with love, support, care, and determination, you can grow to be or do anything you dream of—just like these beans.'"

"I have that kind of faith
and belief in you."

"Keep believing in yourself. Trust in yourself and in all the incredible things you can do.

Dream big,
dear one.
You got this!"

Seeds to Ponder!

Hey readers!

The characters in **The Bean Story** are not the only ones who can discover the fantastic gifts that make them who they are.
You can, too!

Don't forget to ask an adult to join you in this activity.
They can be your garden helper.

Are you ready to dig in?

Great!

Let's get started.

Have you ever wondered about the incredible things that make you unique?

What you like, your talents, your dreams, and things that give you hope or feelings of happiness. They are things that shine bright in your garden. Let's create a GARDEN OF SELF-DISCOVERY to explore and celebrate what makes you unique to help you continue to grow those glimmers of hope and success.

This activity works best with a large piece of paper, but if you don't have one, that's okay! Be creative and unique and use what you have on hand.

NOTE TO ADULTS: This activity encourages children to reflect on their interests, dreams, and what makes them unique. It's a beautiful opportunity for conversations about self-discovery and celebrating each child's individuality.

For this activity you will need:

Blank paper of any colour

Markers, crayons, or coloured pencils

Glue

Scissors

Old magazines, newspapers, or printed pictures

Now let's dig in!

1. Find a cozy space where your creativity can bloom. To help, you could put on some soft music.

2. Put one hand on your belly and one hand on your heart. Take a nice, deep breath in from your belly, close your eyes, and let out your breath. Say, "I am (your name), and I am amazing!" Now open your eyes!

3. Take a moment to think about the things you love, enjoy doing, and dream about. Do you have hobbies, favourite animals, or places you'd like to visit? Are there people you like to spend time with? Think about anything that makes you smile!

4. Draw a big garden box on your blank paper. This is the garden of YOU!

5. Write your name somewhere on the front of the garden box.

6. From the garden box, draw stems for different veggies, fruits, and flowers, or draw the base of a tree.

7. Search for pictures in old magazines, newspapers, or printed images that represent the things you would like to add to your garden.

8. Cut each one out and place them to the side.

9. Now you are ready to plant! Place your pictures at the top of your stems! Remember: Each stem may grow taller or shorter. Just like you, they are unique. Each one might be a different shape, like a flower, vegetable, tree branch, or leaf.

10. What about watering your garden? Drawing raindrops or a watering can with positive words flowing from it can make your garden grow healthy and strong. Maybe some of the words are:
Love
Happiness
Friendship
Peace

11. Do you think it is finished? Do you need to add more? Remember: You can use markers, crayons, or coloured pencils to decorate your garden. Add fun designs and anything that makes it uniquely yours!

12. When you are done, take a step back. Take a big breath in from your belly and let it go. You did a great job! This is your masterpiece. This is YOUR garden, a snapshot of the incredible YOU!

Just like in our story, self-discovery is ongoing. As you grow and experience new things, your garden will change and evolve. It will grow bigger, greener, and stronger. With each new experience you will continue to shine brightly!

Embrace all the fantastic parts of yourself and keep exploring the extraordinary adventure of being YOU!

Feel free to share your GARDEN OF SELF-DISCOVERY with friends and family! Ask an adult if you can also share it on social media using the hashtag #mybeanstory. Let others in on the magic!

Happy growing and discovering!
Dream big, dear ones!
You got this!

Printed in the USA
CPSIA information can be obtained
at www.ICGtesting.com
JSHW070850070624
64381JS00010B/53